T0365620

This book is dedicated to my lovely and wonderful wife, Helene, who with endless patience, support and understanding has allowed me to chase a life in triathlon and help guide my creativity in the sport of triathlon for others to enjoy in the form of children's books.

The active lifestyles we both lead brought us together at a triathlon back in 2001 in Lake Zurich, IL. We married soon afterward and welcomed our first child, Glen James, to the world in December 2003.

What a better way to thank such a lovely woman than with a children's book about the wonderful things she has brought into my life.

To order additional copies of this book, contact:
Xlibris
844-714-8691
www.Xlibris.com
Orders@Xlibris.com

ISBN: Softcover   978-1-4134-7598-2
         Hardcover   978-1-4134-8543-1
         EBook   979-8-3694-3639-4

Print information available on the last page

Rev. date: 12/05/2024

My Triathlon Family

by

Glen McGowean

What a wonderful day.

The sun is shining,
the birds are chirping.

Mommy and Daddy are enjoying this beautiful day exercising.

They bring me with when they can.

I like to cheer them on at Triathlons.

Mommy and Daddy say Triathlon is a lifestyle.

15

They say there is much more to the sport than just swimming, biking and running.

They tell me that I will understand someday.

It's okay that I don't understand.
I like to swim, bike and run.

Someday, I want to do a triathlon with Mommy and Daddy.

23

Someday, Mommy and Daddy will cheer me on at a Triathlon.

25

What a wonderful day.

Printed in the United States
by Baker & Taylor Publisher Services